Uzmah Ali

Breathe Before Thought

First published in 2020
by Waterloo Press (Hove)
95 Wick Hall
Furze Hill
Hove BN3 1NG
Printed in Palatino 10pt by
One Digital
54 Hollingdean Road
East Sussex BN2 4AA

Cover image: © by Neil Alexander.

Author photograph © Uzmah Ali 2020

Uzmah Ali is hereby identified as author of this work in accordance with Section 77 of the Copyright,
Designs and Patents Act 1988

A CIP record for this book is available from the British Library

ISBN: 978-1-906742-94-2

Acknowledgments

Firstly, an acknowledgement to Sufyaan Khaliq, my number one fan. Secondly, to the brilliant community of readers and writers who have been at my side from inception to publication - Shabnam Ahsan, Shahnaz Ahsan, Charissa Fiander, Naomi Foyle, Annabel Gaba, Nargis Ghafoor, Caroline Haffey, Nicki Heinen, Nur Sobers Khan, Summereen Khan, Dr Alan Lane, Kate Leyland, Rukhsana Mannan, Jonathan Palmer, Raha Rafii, Zainab Rahim, Rori Raquib, Mido-Ahmed Waqas and Hesham Zakai.

Also, to Matthew Caley who has been an excellent teacher and an invaluable poetry mentor and introduced me to a vast breadth of possibilities within poetry. Further acknowledgements go to Naomi Foyle and Akila Richards from Waterloo Press for being excellent editors and providing encouragement and support when I needed it most.

Also worthy of mention are Nadia Ameer, Naheed Hussain, Razwana Hussain, Afzana Hussain, Suraya Jina, Rebecca Tucker, and Rachel Davies who have lightened the load with their good company and never-ending laughter. To anyone I have neglected to name, but has had some hand in making this book come to pass, a sincere thank you. I am grateful as well to the Muslim Institute, and of course, Waterloo Press for championing my work.

Finally, an acknowledgement to Neil Alexander for his excellent cover design. His work can be found at neil-alexander.com and @sharkeyed on Instagram.

Dedication:

To The Most High

To my family (5/6)

Asghar Javed Ali
Safia Akhter Ali
Saira Ali
Hamid Raza Ali
Mohsun Hussan Ali

To the countries and histories that made me.

Contents

Stone Circles

One day, my beginning will be
as ancient as the rings of stones
that dot my green nation.

Four Yellow Mounds

the foreign daughter
returns to the dust
four yellow mounds
speak of her own foreignness

these yellow mounds
unmarked
always remembered
fatihah recited

for endings
and beginnings
cupped hands in prayer
a supplicant

her punked hair
under peasant drape
a bashful beg
for belonging

mullah's directives nibble
at her thoughts
telling her to be
better, wiser, chaster

the time for religious
instruction
is gone
she thinks –

in the mist of her mind
like holograms
like faces on stamps
are toothy grins

white lungis, dupattas
kindly, wrinkly hands
caresses
sweet-giving

mum and dad say
let's go
let's fall into the new car
let's fall into new wealth

let's go, let's go

Knot-Welsh-Adults

When it was St David's Day
Everyone else wore the tall felt hat
My Punjabi mother recited high Urdu
And put my school things in my bag.

I turned up in my everyday *dress-pyjamah*
A template from another country
But learnt vocab lists with 'LL' and 'CH' –
She had tied me in my own Welsh Not.

Not that it was intentional
I only understood later
The differences between
Choice, purpose, necessity.

I met a comrade in otherness
From the old book before mine
We exulted in difference
And created a home of our own.

Her dark eyes flashed in the Sabbath lights
I decided she was halfway to understanding me
My adolescent pride hid my tears
As her dad explained Moses
And religious liberty.

We are free men, created by God
The Ten Commandments declared
The film cassette recorded by my father
Told me we are all
Significant, dignified, worthy.

Let me tell you about the ruh, it exists in all
God breathed into Adam, my mum said
Whispering words into the almost darkness
As I slipped into a solid baby-sleep.

I woke to news.
My friend said, 'where were you?'
I was in Chemistry, working on my 'A'
She was in philosophy
Working on life's purpose.

I thought everything would be fine
In the shadow of two shattered towers
Cast long and deformed – across countries,
Touching the Severn Bridge.

We both went to university,
Over the border, got jobs
Existed in the world –
Saw each other grow
Outside of teenage fancies.

Labelled with new coarse knots
We were ignored, slighted,
Passed for promotion
Both hurt, stung, sullied.

5/6 : Family

Silence, SAHYUN
Agonies past
Inform the present

Razed memories
Allowing unfolding
Zion, the new Scion

Make past stranger
"Opportunity"
Silenced

Unremembered
Minute details
Inherent, incipient, still.

Always carry on
Because we can
Unchained

Shall we sing
Our Lord's song
In this strange land?

A Single Stride

In a tableau time out
of history
A farmer, wife, daughter and sons
A turn
of events, and a son
had to leave

*

He traversed epochs
and continents
in a single stride
and made it
look so easy
Ghalib and Iqbal had saturated
his monsoon air
and now his daughter learns
about Shakespeare
'…did Shakespeare write poems, as well as plays, then?'
On a cold afternoon
in a trendy uniform
in a classroom
in a Welsh comp
in English Literature
her black eyelashes blink
tears
Because Othello and Shylock have spoken
If you tickle us, do we not laugh?

*

She remembers how
he taught her
to be
self-taught

She begins to learn
of the unspoken
epics behind her father's eyes
that she will
never understand
And he understands
And she understands
In the familiar comfort
of silence
they both understand.

Pomegranates in Lahore

In my Khala's house in Lahore
my sister holds a large pomegranate.
The fruit, a pinkish yellow, mottled grey
garnished with a perfect round crown.

I know there is a history here,
we are near the Wagah border.
My mother says we are her miracles,
we are her bucheh, raanis and rajahs.

My sister cuts the fruit and swears in English.
Finally a rough and enforced incision.
She puts her finger in the dark crack,
and pulls the fruit away in two parts.

There's a minute, gentle, agonised creak
and a small groan, an acute shudder.
The little red seeds convulse in an arc,
scatter everywhere against their will.

I scrabble on my knees and pick them up.
I hold one to the light: almost perfect,
a soft curve on its edges, glowing rose,
the seed is floating in the middle of the gem,

an organic ruby, a tiny embryo,
living, floating, next to lots of others.
The fine barrier between them, a pale yellow,
a lipid you might consume to respire.

Some have been crushed under my weight,
burst underfoot, leaving a residue,
soon to be rancid, tacky and sickly
Hues of bloodiness in a battle scene.

Holding the half sphere over a large bowl
my sister hits the fruit hard with a spoon.
Seeds fall out slowly and reluctantly
in the white pyrex that is not their home.

They are divided, to be consumed.
Their destiny is brutal, random, unfair.
I eat the seeds feeling grit in my mouth.
The juice leaves a tartness on my tongue.

Khwajasarah Songs

the songs are practised,
light and drifty, harmonious
notes float up to houses.

we are sitting rooftop in Lahore
here for family weddings
witness to customs,

in textbooks, lectures,
things I've only ever heard of,
here like a living

archive of motifs.
they sing and we smile
moths of notes rising

in flutter, spiral
all around. they smile, kohl eyes, lips
reshmi clothes, make up,

my youthful zeal
would have seen sin
where there is none

now: breathe before thought.

Beyond People

In a place beyond books
Where the people are broken
But still breathing
Where the air is full of colour

The words are full of creation
I walked ancient paths in search of truth

The old woman was preaching under a scatter of roses petals

The otherness, psychedelic, iridescent, present
The otherness, in between, beyond, everywhere
The otherness, living, watching, always here

I turned to leave. I was frightened
But then I turned back. She taught me how to be free.

So I thought.

The frayed satin itched against my arms
From the walls of my prison cell
I heard the gun click

Village Girl Lights

Sat together, the light blazes
They see shapes not seen before,
When daylight slowly faded.

She teaches her brother letters,
Knowledge unknown
To mum, dad, kin and clan.

She is the first to unlock
Symbols that determine fates
In law codes and assemblies.

Before wires snaked the wall
And bulbs dangled like fruit
Reading was dusked by dark.

He recalls clearly
His heart would sadden
At black receding ink.

He is learning now:
Letters make words, minds,
No longer to the sun's rules.

Side by side they read,
Under the new light.

On the Excellence of Hyphens

Testimony of a Welsh-Woman in Pakistan:
My movements are monitored
My speech assessed
The weight of history falls, itchy on my skin.

Testimony of a Welsh-Pakistani Woman in Lahore:
There is comfort in the lens of kanals
Smokiness from childhood adventures
Arriving in a half-known language.

Testimony of a British-Asian in London:
We've been etched here for centuries
Engraving continents with spice and cotton –
Now, people take sandpaper to our marks.

Testimony of a Pakistani-Welsh Woman in Lahore:
I dreamt of going to university here
But at present it is the site of family holidays
I bestow on my children my former dreams.

Quiet

Quiet times enraged the heart
The heart where she lived
Outside she was virtue

Silent times enraged the heart
The heart where she lived
Outside she was pliant

There were times when she didn't matter

To move from one geography, one ownership, one life
As adept as a blacksmith or carpenter in skill
A plaster cast of survival

Then she was allowed to speak
Only to be told that her words
Were of an age that was no more.

Conversation with a Shop Assistant

She is distant, gruff. She doesn't like me. Because of my olive skin, because of my headscarf? I can't be sure. But, tis the season. I chide myself for my morbidity.   Jihadi attack, thirty-two dead in Brussels. People will hate me for a while. Seasonal, a poisonous thaw. What is she thinking? How dare I shop, smile, laugh, work, love! An unjust entitlement. Her response to my question about dress sizes is reluctant, like the oozing of sloppy concrete. For an instant I wonder what it would be like to look like her. Pale, blonde, blue eyed. What would it be like not to worry about frosty stares, hesitant conversation, racist kicks and punches? Would it be a liberation?   No. It would be the enslavement of engineered ignorance.

Political Rap Gig

The hip-hop beats pump in the dark basement. We all dance. I think I smell booze, sweet and rancid. I wonder if I'll ever get used to the smell? In unison, our arms swaying, a limb-filled tide. Fuck the system. Fuck capitalism. Fuck white supremacy. This is third world democracy. A giant cluster of heads. Afros, Hijabs, Indian Hair, Far Eastern Hair, Long, Wiry, Curly, Cropped, Coloured. Here, we can be ourselves. My hijab obscures my vision. I have lost my friend. He has gone to get a pint and tap water for me. He's easy enough to spot in the crowd. Tall, blond, clean shaven, wearing a 'Free Palestine' t-shirt.

Fragment of Cloth in Llangorse Lake

There is a fragment of cloth
From long ago
Woven deeply within me.

I imagine I can feel
The crosshatch of stitch
Over the fine and ancient weave.

Maybe a queen was touched
By the hands of a woman
I might recognise as my own.

Dubrovnik

There are marble streets here
Palisades, towers
Cliffs that fall into the sea

The women wear heels or walking shoes
Retirees, couples on honeymoon
Kayaking on the Adriatic

Palm and pomegranate scent
The late summer sun is warm
Like skin, kisses, sweat

We walked the perimeter
A bolstered fortress
The red sunset flecking the waves

There is a room on the corner
Where screams are trapped in photos
Framing humanity's sin

Gaping mouths, sallow, gaunt
Guns, smoke, khaki
Primal fear, crosshair fire

The landmarks, in another life
Are amber, searing, hellish
Through grey-smoke-haze

There are depraved whispers
I strain to hear
I try to understand

With my Euros in my pocket
Tucked tightly
In my red tourist card.

Srebrenica

Our tour guide leaves us
The group dissipates
And treads the gentle curve of lush green hills
With occasional traffic gliding past
Marking the languid drift of time and space
Small white pillars dot the hills as far as the eye can see
The wrap of the Ottoman turban placed on top
The decoration of dignity
Born in 1981, it says, he was 14
I want to hug all the gravestones
I want to touch each one
Put my cheek to the cool marble of every white pillar
I'm sorry, I'm sorry, I'm sorry
The only words that surface in my mind.

A Surprise Donation

The books of a deceased person; I assumed a man, because the books are doused in the tar touch of a cigar smoker, the edges sepia yellow. Dostoyevsky, Hobsbawm, Rousseau, Marx. The books arrive when I am seventeen, and desperate to become worldly. History dictates that I should be cheated out of letters. Instead, my parents make a nest of books. The books find pride of place on MFI linoleum. Maybe women can smoke cigars too? Each time I turn a page, I learn a new way to breathe.

Learning

Education. Dickens. Shakespeare. Marlowe.
Never Tagore, Spivak or Ghalib.
Education. The Tudors, World War II, the Holocaust.
Not the kids' infinite unnamed dead.
Always great white men, intellectual sharks
The kids shrunk away from pedigree's shore.
Those were hobbies they couldn't afford,
Hobbies they didn't want or need to do.
'Learn the technical, mathematical
Subjects; teaching you how to be someone –
Someone who will be better than you.'
Some would use the novel pen fluently;
Others would draw jagged staccato lines.
Some sat in school, glazed, indifferent.
Would they be acknowledged?
Ever important?

Roseh/ Ramzan /Ramadhan

Walk out into the evening
Feel the murmur of the breeze
On your parched and tired face.

Stars begin to speckle the purple sky
Eat your meal
You have communed with poverty.

Not Praying Taravih in Ramzan

I'm not reading, but I can watch and listen
Absorb and be blessed

Everyone is rising and falling in unified purpose
I wonder how many wishes have come true in the blessed month
How many prayers have been answered

I don't understand the recitation
Apart from a few snatched words
From Arabic lessons I forgot

Undulating cadence, divine poetry
The rustle of Gore-Tex, the hum of air conditioning
The male congregants on screen
A mirror image of movement

Back to the liturgy I know
The penta
A long ameen I join in an act of clandestine rebellion
I need to stop listening to punk music

God listens to those who pray
Everyone drops
Then they greet the celestial beings
Look over the right shoulder, and the left
Almost like checking blind spots

I'm tired of standing
I lean my back against the small cupboard door
On the periphery of the prayer hall
And slide down until I'm sitting on the floor

I am in an upright foetal position
Knees pushed against my chest
Maybe my first position as I fell into this world

There is a muffled noise, a sob or a sneeze
Someone is crying, or has a cold
I can't tell

The ladies' feet are covered in the length of their abayahs
They are all frozen in prostration
The only flesh I can see the soles of a man's feet
On the video cast from the men's hall
They look soft, adept in an act of prayer
Tucked under his frame, close together
As he bends in a considered sajood.

To me he will forever be a stranger
Joined in the intimacy of prayer.

Occupy when occupied

How many times have you heard
Quiet murmurings in the night
Of repugnance from a former age
Requesting you to disappear?

This space is yours
Unfold absolutely

Do not let them tell you
How to be

Own absolutely.

Notes

Four Yellow Mounds. Fatihah is the first section of the Quran which is often recited at weddings, funerals, and when offering condolences to the family of the deceased.

Knot-Welsh-Adults. The Welsh Not was an item used in Welsh schools between the 18ᵗʰ and 20ᵗʰ centuries to stigmatise and punish children using the Welsh language. It was typically a length of rope tied to a wooden placard engraved with the letter WN. It was worn around the neck and was passed from child to child during the school day as they were caught speaking Welsh. The last child wearing the item at the end of the school day would be punished.

Dress-pyjamah is a term used in the Punjabi Muslim diaspora that describes what young girls would wear to school. Western dresses would be accompanied by a 'pyjamah'. The pyjamah would be a cotton trouser, often homemade, cut in the Punjabi style. By wearing a pyjamah under a dress, the Punjabi Muslim cultural preference for the covering of legs as a mark of honour and modesty would be fulfilled.

Ruh is a theological concept within Islam which has similarities with the Holy Spirit in Christianity. Muslims hold that Allah or God breathed into the material body of Adam (peace be upon him), the first human, and by extension, the breath of God that animated Adam in the first instance, continues to exist in all people.

Khwajasarah Songs. Khwajasarah is an Urdu word, that refers to the transgender community in Pakistan. The community is associated with providing entertainment at weddings.

Fragment of Cloth in Llangorse Lake. An archaeological find in Llangorse Lake, near the Brecon Beacons is widely believed to be the remains of a 9th century royal residence in Wales with international connections. The site contained fragments of cloth that were embellished with silk that may have come from somewhere on the silk road, perhaps Persia or as far afield as China. The cloth is believed to have formed part of a tunic worn by Welsh royalty. A detail of the cloth is depicted on the front cover.

Not Praying Taravih in Ramzan. The Taravih prayer is an additional prayer, prayed every evening of Ramzan, the holy month of fasting. The prayer is added onto the last obligatory prayer of the day. Women are excluded from prayer in the event of their monthly period, on account of ritual impurity. In this case, it is common for women to attend congregational prayers, and sit quietly on the periphery of the prayer and observe, rather than take part in the formal congregation.